Jack's road

"Look at my road,"

said Jack.

"My car is on the road,"

said Jack.

"Can my bus go

on the road?"

said Billy.

Glue

"Look at my bus!"

said Billy.

"Can my bus go

on the road?"

said Billy.

"My car is on the road,"

said Jack.

"My truck is on the road,"

said Jack.

"My **bus** is on the road,"

said Billy.